Somewhere Through the Haze

By Analysis

Eliza:
Thank you so much, fellow poet,
for your ear and spirit and
support!

Peace, Justice, Poetry!
Analysis

Poetic Vibe
4/15/22

© 2019 by Analysis (Kenneth R. Brown)
ISBN 978-0-359-82080-1

Publisher: Simply Poetic Press

Front cover photo: "Contemplation--Books and Coffee," by Stephanie Chapman, for the collection "More Than Words"
Back cover photo by Stephanie Chapman
https://sweetturtleberry.com/

Book design by Simply Sherri,
www.simplypoeticentertainment.com

TABLE OF CONTENTS

PREFACE

I often tell people that I'm surprised I fell into poetry as late in life as I did. When, in my 40s, I finally did get onto the spoken word scene, I found it to be a natural artistic outlet for my soul, for my love of language and, most certainly, for my examination of justice issues and my desire for a transformed world. The poems in this collection are a reflection of that desire. I hope they raise within you key questions, spur you to further learning, provide opportunity for lively discussion, and help motivate you to action so that we may, indeed, achieve that transformed world.

Too many to name here are the family, friends and fellow poets who have supported me, all of whom have my love and gratitude. I must, however, acknowledge my friend and poetic colleague Simply Sherri for her invaluable assistance in the production of this book.

Analysis
Baltimore, Maryland, USA 2019

IMMIGRATION ACROSTIC

Asinine interjections of anti-immigrant hate create
Bathos to any expectation of intelligent thought
Coming from those who, in their own insecurities,
Denigrate those who cross oceans and
Cross burning deserts, having been
Excluded from all that mutual wealth
Free trade agreements egregiously guaranteed.
Greed runs rampant as big bosses make profits while
Hypocritical descendants of immigrants clamor about an
Imagined invasion, their ignorance exceedingly ugly.
Jokes are played on folks from
Around the world who anticipated
Kind and warm welcome to this "land of the free."
Labor under-rewarded is order of the day,
Manipulated by rulers of capital who capitalize off the
Need of poor folk and refugees to
Replenish their children's bellies,
Or remit something home to stave off starvation.
Prejudice is prescribed through
Parapets and prohibitive policies.
Queries as to how we might best
Welcome our new neighbors are deflected by
Restrictionists who reroute public thought with
Lies of how immigration,
Supposedly, steals from "our" surplus and
Sacks "our" social order.
Those tainted by Tanton tout English-only as
The only acceptable form of communication, and
Undervalue ethnic studies which enhance a healthy society.
My people:
Void from your souls all such vitriol against those who arrive!
White America is threatened, in the minds of the haters, and
Xenophobic fear is what they will tempt you to.
You, however, must remain wise to such lies, and permit
Zero tolerance for hate against the newcomer in this place!

RECRUITMENT

And tell me: when you kill her, what will it feel like?

Will you delight in the touch of your finger against the trigger
That dispatches death to one designated discardable
Due to her presence in an "enemy combatant zone?"
Will you sense the softness of her skin as it's
Severed by your 7.62, and attune yourself to
The intonation of her aorta torn asunder,
Calling into question the caliber of your character as you
Chamber another round of red, white and blues
For an occupied people to moan?
In your fervor to hunt her husband and persecute her parents
As you do what your bosses taught 'cha,
Will you use the lessons offered
Down in Georgia at the School of Torture?
Will you gorge her, or maybe
Torch her and her village because they have the misfortune of
Looking like this mysterious thing called "the enemy?"
Or will you just fly the drones that terrorize towns and
Make for the stuff of nightmares as everyday folk shudder at
The everyday chance of fire falling from the nighttime sky?
And what of the children?
What of their nighttime cries as their terrorized minds
Try to understand why another friend dies,
Why they grow up having to hide,
When it will all end,
When they will be next...

When you rape her, what will it sound like?

Will the soul-chilling screams of
Her soul being snatched as your spoils of war
Stay with you long after your "unit" has moved on?
Will you wonder if she'll be able to move on from
The "Freedom" the great western saviors assaulted her with,
Or how long it will take her to wash off

4

The stench of your occupation?
Is this part of the protecting, when you
Ghraib all you can and ride roughshod over
God's other children?
What of her children?
Will your violations give volition to the
Violence they'll commit trying to process terrible shit done,
PTSD piercing their sanity deeply, as it will yours?
Exactly whose voices do you think they'll listen to next—
Those that groan in uninvited
Enjoyment of their mothers and aunts,
Or those that whisper into their ears that they have
Nothing left to lose so they might as well run kilos or
Strap 20 sticks to themselves and
Take as many out of this fucked-up life with them as they can?

You on that shit, ain't you?
That drug of patriotism, boosted by lack of opportunity and
Laced with the lure of adventure,
As if you get to enlist in some real-life PlayStation®.
You feel it's your call of duty to
Strong-arm countries for your superiors,
Sensing something is sour about the situation;
Still you stick to your assassin's creed only to discover that
The mettle of your honor is sorely tested by the
Less than honorable role this country
Plays on the world stage.
Thus, you find yourself in the company of heroes
Whose actions got staged by the system.
You see, this is real life.
You don't get any extra lives, just extra lies and
Extra ties to the gears of war,
But this modern warfare can
Shred your soul into splinter cells,
Leaving you wondering how you lost your halo as you
Look back over the marred battlefield your life has become.

You're so eager to put yourself at risk—
Like a little plastic piece on a board game.
The boards are game for you tame their markets so they
Roll the dice with your sacrifice and
Make sound nice the dicier parts of this life,
All so that you'll go and make the world safe for democracy—
Or rather safe for undemocratic regimes and
Corporate interests that don't work corporately
With the people's interests.
This "liberation" you bring them is paid for with high interest.
I'm interested in knowing if any of this caught your interest
Or were you uninterested in knowing, refusing to take a
Closer look at the ground truth before you
Hit the ground running.
Yours not to reason why; yours but to do—
A die coming up sixes for the rulers' tricks and
Snake eyes for your spirit's serenity.

You say, "it's won't happen to me."
And when it does you can say you were
Simply following orders to aim high, and you did—
Shooting low the hopes and dreams of people
Across the globe, so now you're a global force.
For good or for bad, you decided to be all you could be
In the employ of the empire but now you're
Searching for the things that made it all worthwhile
And finding them few, the proud moments rare.
Over there you'll handle million-dollar machinery
But the machine back home doesn't handle you with trust
So it's a bust. You can return home
To be on the front lines for your family's food assistance.
I hope you don't return home cuttin' lines,
Or wheelin' in line at the VA looking for spare parts.
Indeed, I just hope you return home.

Look, I don't claim to have easy answers or
A job in my pocket. Guess you figure there ain't much hirin';
School ain't firin' on all cylinders so you say "why not?"
That's what they're counting on:
People of color and poor whites to give up the fight
And give themselves up to fight. Right, right—
I know we all have service people in our families.
We love them very much, would very much love for them
Not to be taken away from our families
Or to take people away from theirs.
I'm aware some of my own support branches down
From the branches and from the making of arms
But that doesn't mean I can treat this at arm's length,
So I'm arming you with ammo to make an informed decision
Before you choose to be uniformed into uniformity.
This military industrial complex is making life complex.
So, at the risk of your being vexed, I offer questions
You must consider Before you consider
The taking of others' lives or, possibly, your own.
Will you own your path or merely march down one
On orders to disorder another's? Young brother,
I'm not trying to run your life or cause unnecessary strife...

...But I'm just wondering:
When you beat her, what will she cry like?

Will she shout shrieks of terror, shocked that
The man she wedded is now wedded to
Imbedding his fist in her,
Your bedding now a battleground brought home?
Or, in hushed trembling, will she stream the slow, steady,
Almost quiet tears of a woman quietly resigned to
This new prison of a life, her personal Guantanamo
Where she's force-fed fear, seasoned with memories of
What used to be that keep her
Caged in a deranged domestic detainment.
A part of you died over there
And you try to drink away the damnable parts that didn't but

All you cause is dread in a domicile where happiness is dead.
Will you remember your happiness when you first knew
You loved her,
Her smile when you blew your first kiss?
Now your blows don't miss! You've blown your bliss,
Shelled all of this into a shell of what you had back then.
Son, what of your children?
Will your son learn from you how to disable an opponent,
Even one dearly beloved?
He'll want to be in the strike force, like Daddy.
Will he strike with force, like Daddy,
Landing shells upon a woman he'll reduce to a shell?
Will your daughter be shell shocked into
Shelving her sense of self-worth and succumbing to the hell
Some similarly sick bastard will sentence her to?

Salute the God within before you salute the gods of war, and
Think on these things before you sign on the dotted line—
Just above the perforation of your soul from its peace.

So everyone was on a rainbow high,
Caught up in the swirl of all the colors
That were to unfurl evenly, dreamily,
Promising you and me that society would be as it should be,
That we could all be together on life's playground and that
Everyone would play real nice.
Thing is, we got played—real nice.
Let ourselves get caught napping so heavily that
The dream got blurred
And the wisdom of the dream weaver got obscured,
And in our grogginess we miss how much
Our dream's been abjured.

Our King decreed that we should be vigilant and
Heed his warnings sent from the court of a
Birmingham jail, and scribed in *Why We Can't Wait*. [1]
But it seems we've waited things out long enough to
Let the enemies at the gate attack our royal sage,
Assuaging us by promoting him to demigod and thus
Demoting him and his prophetic power.
We nod, dozing as a still-hateful world has us
Join hands and say "I have a dream,"
While ignoring the edgier incisiveness of the Dreamer.
You see, their scheme was brilliant:
Have us happy for a holiday and
Placate us with a few morsels of rights
While right in front of our eyes they continue to feast on
Elaborate systemic racism and
Extravagant economic exploitation,
Discarding justice as waste for disposal,
Washed away with a watered-down view of Martin—
A sad reality in a supposed dream world.
Reality is, you don't hear them holla in
Support of our support of black dollars.
With stealth they suppress the wealth ML wanted us to build,
Undercutting our understanding of the *ujamaa* in his

Urgent calls for unified action. You don't hear
Abundant accolade for his address of April 4, '67—
A year to the day before a bullet sent him to heaven for
Denouncing the hell this country raised in Southeast Asia.
They'd rather keep us dreaming in fantasia than
For us to wake up, knowing that it's "time to break silence."

Public perception is stuck on the steps of the Memorial,
Memorialized, i.e., dead—or so it would seem. Thus,
I have a dream, deferred.
Not that I'm not proud of
The spectacular speech in front that crowd.
Indeed, it's good to see the props our leader and elder
So deservedly receives. However, we're deceived
If we think his fuller message of equality is
Fully believed or if such is even close
To having been achieved. So be careful of
Hollow hosannas and loosely-thrown laudation;
Not everyone who says of him, "Lord, Lord"
Wants to enter the King-dom.

Still, for a few days every middle of January we get
Inundated with effusive exaltation and
Empty exclamations about keeping the dream alive
From a society that continues to kill it,
Keeping itself exempt of any responsibility to fulfill it,
While those non-exempt from being "the other"
Work hard with no benefits of privileged status.
So while the privileged deify the Drum Major for Justice,
They keep folk dragging their feet to
The drone of a conformist beat that
Drums into our heads a dumbed-down version of the
Radical strive toward freedom he lead us on.

Of course, we do have MLK Boulevards
Across the urban landscape,
Some in areas that would make the honoree cringe
At the dishonorable conditions he sought to eradicate.
He would hate the under-resourcing of

Many schools bearing his name. Elementary inequities in
Line items and allotments help establish
A secondary education so exiguous of equal footing that
The erudite ecclesiastic would eschew association with
The eponymous engravings on the edifices.

Yet, when the celebrations have ceased and we declare
Our continued concerns about our
Continued confinement to a lower caste,
We are condescendingly told, "Awww—that was cute!
Now run a long and play;
We have more important things to do, like
Control the wealth and build our empire.
Why don't you go build a campfire and sing
'Kum Bah Yah, my Lord'? Just don't come by here."
My Lord, I wonder when we'll be
Free at last, free at last from falling for the false reverence
This country offers the Reverend as these felons feign
To affirm the transformation of society he fought for,
Frontin' just far enough to finagle our favor and
Force their fingers into our fortune!
Unfortunately, the chaos in our community
Accommodates this fraud as we
Fail to focus on where we go from here.

He said, "I may not get there with you, but...
We as a people will get to the Promised Land!"
Seems we've landed on promises, promises,
Settling for a promissory note from a nation that
Promised us a story denoted by justice but instead
Wrote more bad checks 'cause
We still don't receive much credit in this union.
So here's a reality check:
Our dream is the oppressors' nightmare because
Sharing the power and the purse scares them to death and so
They make sure we stay asleep, deep in REM stage as
They stage peaceful scenes for our matrix,
Making us think we've made it and that
Martin's work is done.

Everybody was on a rainbow high,
Caught up in the swirl while
Those who have no love for the Beloved Community
Loved watching it crash low. We better act like we know:
The only way the dream will come true is for us to
Wake up, and get real.
And somewhere through the haze,
a prophet still points the way forward.
Maybe we'll get the point, and keep moving.

[Inspired in part by a painting by CHOKE
(Creating Her Own Kinetic Energy @cho_ke right)]

THE CELLING OF SOULS

Paul and Silas, bound in jail,
Sing God's praise both night and day
And I hope dat trump might blow me home
To the new Jerusalem! [2]

I hope it does blow them home,
All those seized in the marketplace of human capital.
But right now all I hear trumpeted are blustering boasts
About being tough on crime, and misleading media made to
Maintain some manufactured "war on drugs"
That keeps officials chasing the scream of those in need
While ignoring their cries for help.

Thus, cells swell; more dwell in them here in the
"Land of Liberty" than anywhere else.
Even the smallest or most repented-for of offenses could
Get you penned up in a maze of mandatory minimums.
This mandates a story; at minimum a telling of truth
'Cause this situation keeps many doing time,
And "time keeps on slipping into the future." [3]
We want to fly like an eagle but all we see is
The new "Jim Crow" in a societal cage with
Human rights perverted in the presence of the Most High,
Human nights deserted, people missing; broken families cry.
Millions on the inside, near forgotten. Do we ask why?
Seems like folk could care less how they got there
Or if numbers die in deplorable conditions,
Their lamentations being met with lamentable lies.
Oh, the rulers speak pretty words about equal justice but
Modify their verbs to contain no action.
Their sentence structure is unbalanced,
With a bias renowned that predicates a belief that
People of color and poor white subjects are to be
Relegated to a subordinate clause. Pardon my grammar, but
That "ish" just ain't right, and the only "corrections" I see
Are the glaring ones that need to be made to

This criminal injustice system.
Both public and privatized prisons are
Run like rental companies where individuals are
Treated as junk for storage.
This arrangement might find you hauled away
But this ain't mom's Attica.
It's the san-quintessential squelching of souls, with
No renaissance of freedom in Florence;
More like the crucifixion of lives, an Angola Three up on
Crosses constructed of falsehood, fear and greed.
Even the Nazarene would catch the Folsom prison blues
Under these conditions. Imagine if the Carpenter had to
Sing, sing a song of stolen liberties.
Countless commune in his name, but act as if
The least of these are mere un-leaven, worth passing over.

Take those 2.2 million of the Creator's loved ones
Locked up in the U.S. Add them to the
21 million of God's children—many just children—
Carted around the world as chattel,
Driven by the trade in forced sex and labor,
And you've got gridlock on the road to any rights,
With nobody moving freely.
Up next: human traffic, and whether or not
You choose to reroute your eyes around it, it's still there.

Wonder why this absurdity is so out-of-control?
Follow the money. The prison industrial
Isn't that complex when its context is clarified as
Corporate players monopolizing human beings like
Tokens after they land on "go to jail."
It's easier to figure when you factor in the foolishness of
Police districts getting bonuses for
Blowing up their bookings and filling beds.
See, this is slavery by any other name—
Oh, wait: the loophole in the 13th does call it that, doesn't it?
Well, there it is, easy as one, two, three:
The strikes you get before you're struck
Out of the full roster of citizenship,

Sent down to the minors,
Disenfranchised.

You don't even get that many swings if you're the away team
Trying to play in the home park of the privileged.
Hard-working folk forced to flee their forebears' farms due to
Falling prices fashioned by "free trade," or
Fleeing violent factions fueled by arms
Forged in northern factories and Faustian pacts
Between our Federal and its nefarious friends.
Thousands go through hell to get here only to arrive in hell.
Surprised? Well, you won't hear tell of this too much.
Our "welcoming" government quells this,
Trying to keep it on the sly,
But now detention is a family affair, with everyday people
Rounded up together then torn apart—
Parents and children made separate, but
Equal is the pain in their hearts.
They were hoping this country would want them to stay but
They found out that even here not everybody is a star.
For them there's no hot fun in the summertime 'cause
They got ICE'd. So while they're made to
Dance to the music of orchestrated racism,
They look for allies to help take them higher. Question is,
Will we stand with them, doing what we can so
Their God-given dignity is respected and
They can be themselves again?

We must be the ones that make this earth quake!
We must be the trumpets that make walls shake with justice
That opens doors and blows the captives home!
Indeed, we might be the next captives.
So we either lock arms with those on lockdown
Or our spirits languish.
Our action is of seismic importance; we'd better not blow it.

I'm not sure which I find most amusing,
In a sick kind of way—
What embarrassed response you invoke,
When we invite you to rethink these ill names and logos,
I find most ludicrous.

Perhaps it's the way, outside the stadiums, that you
Scurry away like guilty mice and
Bypass a brochure or a word of advice on why
Your conduct connotes ignorance, as if your
Consciences becoming conscious were
A trap to be averted for dear life.
Alerted to the mere tripe in your tainted minds,
We offer another view but your fear makes fools of you.
Your down-low hate rises to the top and
Pours over sickeningly, like beer spilled by
Frenzied fans drunk on large drafts of white privilege,
Served with an order of caste order in which
Indigenous are the most ignored
Except in some twisted parody.
I saw a father damn near hurt his son
Snatching a flier out of his hand and thus
Hurting his child's mind,
Snatching out of it inquisitiveness and a willingness to learn.
This inquisition on understanding will spurn any sense of the
Respect folk should be teaching their children to show.

Maybe it's when you yell "Go home!"
News flash: Native Americans ARE home!
But since your minds are framed by this country's
Founding pillars of genocide, land theft and forced labor
You labor to confess your culture banditry,
Making this mascot matter more than just
a mountain out of a molehill—

Which brings me to this profundity: "We're honoring them!"
Right. Your clownish chants and stereotyped images are
The example of adoration, aren't they?
Your belittling caricatures and wannabe "warpaint"

Reveal such reverence;
Your fake feathers confer such homage upon
Sacred symbols and spiritual paths…
Enough of your patronizing nonsense!
You say it's all in fun. Tell me:
Fun at whose expense? Your retaliation would be intense
If the roles were reversed but since this country
Re-versed real history into a set of lies its first nations get to
Lie real low in this current one's level of comprehension.
I guess it's easier to have fun when you
Contort a people into some cartoonish concoction
Created by your conquer-at-all-cost world view.
"What's in a name," you ask as you shake spears that
Slice the self-image of native youth and give them one more
Reason to consider slicing life blood from themselves
To avoid being infused with more of
The poison this society pumps them with.

For five centuries open hunting on native culture
Has been in regular season
And now you strive to make the play off somebody's soul,
Your own having played off
Any remorse over the ridicule you spew.
This negative, knucklehead nomenclature is a national crime.
Thus, in DC we see a capital offense:
The commemoration of cruelty
Cloaked in the cries of fanatics who think they merely name
A team and a "race" but instead name a
Barbarism elevated to genocidal practice by colonists,
Scalping being more than just the
Extortionist resale of tickets.
Charging for this torturous retail was routine:
40£ for a man's red skin, 20 for a woman's or child's.
I wonder how much it cost you to cut your mind off from
Your soul then sell them both.

It seems this shallowness is spread across the land like some
Manifest Destiny of defamation.
In an Erie move settlers went wahoo
And cleaved land away from Ohio's originals.
Folks down in Florida state they cleared it with the tribe but
They only semi-know the story,
Ignoring an exiled nation that remains
Exiled from the decision-making process.
You see, Toto, you're not in Kansas anymore—unless your
Chief mission is shooting dignity out the sky like
Black Hawk down. So I wonder: are there those in Atlanta
Brave enough to break away from this buffoonery,
Or will this country just keep dancing at halftime,
Putting the "tomahawk chop" to the
Chimera of cultural concern it claims to celebrate?

Euro ethnic groups, you ought to know better
After what you endured coming to this country,
But now that you're not at the back of the line
You find time to taunt others.
What really boggles my mind is black folk
Buying into this bullshit, burying any memory
Of the mockeries we were made to endure.
How quickly we forget,
Even though our family vines intertwine deeply with the
First communities of these western continents.
Scarcely can I remember my great-grandmother's hair
Or my grandmother's eyes and countenance
The contempt that resides in yours.
Don't stare at me with some indignant frown,
'Cause you know damn well
If the stadium were for the Washington "Darkies"
We'd have burnt that shit down!
So let this shit burn down into you
Until you reconsider your views, as I had to.
See, I had to realize there were real people
On the other side of my dramatics.
My asinine antics went unabated

Until my assimilating ass was appropriately advised—
And now I'm telling you.

But some of y'all still ain't hearing me.
So I guess that after heads on pikes and severed limbs,
Abusive schools for children to fear,
Poxed-up blankets and fucked-over treaties,
Sand Creek and the Trail of Tears
That it's OK to add insult to injury by insisting on
Imbecilic symbols and team names
That insulate this society from
Any acknowledgment of its anti-indigenous injustice.
We finally got rid of "Little Black Sambo"
And the "Frito® Bandito" but this
Cherokee® driving,
Apache® flying,
Red Man® chewing,
Crazy Horse® drinking country
Still barks out sickening slurs for you to slurp up
At the stadium and be part of the product shot
For a white-normative world.
Any person with a sensitive soul would sense this
And step back from it,

But maybe you're not a person; just a mascot.
So keep cheering, and wait 'till it's
Your turn on the season's schedule to be reduced to a joke.
And when it is, enjoy the game.

POEM FOR THE COALITION OF IMMOKALEE WORKERS

As I bite into a delicious Jubilee
I'm forced to wonder if the person who picked it is even free.
You see, I grew up with the noble images of
Those who collected the fruit of the earth,
In idyllic scenes perfected by a peaceful farming life;
No oppression, no strife.
At least that's what they told us.
Brainwashed us with some wholesome images;
A bill of goods they sold us
'Cause the goods they sell us often come to us
Through a pain they don't tell us about;
So when the workers cry out, we react with doubt.
Finding it hard to believe that
What we buy from our supermarket isn't always retrieved
With the due respect we thought all farmworkers received.
But, for real—this isn't *Green Acres* or *Hew Haw*, yall;
This ain't the *Little House on the Prairie*
Or even *Smallville*; naw, [4]
This is how most of our food gets to our plate,
Through this county's traditional estate of
Labor exploitation cultivated in hate.

A Steinbeck scene put into current context;
I never could have guessed what would be next.
Human beings being stressed by oppressors,
Stomped like grapes of wrath run through presses
Weighted down by pails of 30-plus pounds!
Long, backbreaking days and incessant rounds
Of picking those green, red-orange delectables
That we find so acceptable to be on our plates, bountiful,
The corporation unaccountable.

Statue says, "Give me your…masses yearning to be free."
Seems to be a lie to me
'Cause if you don't look like one of the dominant culture,
But have a hue more like some of you or me,
You might be yearning for a freedom you can't see.

Free trade agreements give the poor
The "freedom" of starvation
Or of sending a loved one off to a plantation
For slave wages, welcomed with greetings
Of locks and chains, pistol whippings and beatings.
Workers putting lives at stake for a beefsteak!
The bosses know what they're doing; it's no mistake.
They're more interested in the quantity of their
Better Boys and Big Girls than in the quality conditions
That would allow workers' children to be better boys,
Or grow up to be big girls.

"You say tomato, I say tomato;" [5]
Corporations say the same old bullshit bravado,
Creating a mix of publicity and tricks
With which to confuse the public's wits;
Concealing the public's knowledge of
The battering and the sticks.
Making a profit off the public's ignorance is
How they get their kicks!
Tricking the public into hopping on over to where
Shopping is a pleasure—
As long as you don't measure the blood, sweat and tears
Harvested in this treasure that supports executive leisure.

However, the workers! Now, collectively,
The workers grow stronger, like a fine wine, and so
We follow their leadership,
Ally with them, knowing that over time
Justice will prevail in the fields and
Human rights will be deemed
More important than what a crop yields.

Their spirit is strong, and even in the midst of tears
They sing freedom songs.
So, with them, we continue the Struggle.
Though the road may be long,
Integrity is ours, and to us the victory belongs! So...

Kultivate, mwen v' swete fos te a pou ou!
Kultivate, mwen v' swete fos te a pou ou!
Trabajadores, que la fuerza de la tierra es suya!
Trabajadores, que la fuerza de la tierra es suya!
Farmworkers, may the strength of the earth be yours!
Farmworkers, may the strength of the earth be yours!
Coalition, may the strength, may the strength,
May the strength of the earth be yours!

*[Written and first performed for the Farmworkers
Freedom March, Tampa, Florida, April 18, 2010.
For more information on the Coalition of
Immokalee Workers, visit www.ciw-online.org]*

POEM FOR JARREL

"My hands are down; my hands are down!"

That's what I head he said,
Before the metal darts bore into him,
Before all that current tore in through him. 50,000 volts—
Not once, but twice, causing a schism in his
Neural and cardiac system. Let's do the division:
100,000 by 20 years of a young black man's life.
That would be 5,000 units of hate for each year
He had to live with the stress and strife
Of being a young African in a society full of
Banality and police brutality,
A society of racial profiling, subtly smiling,
Thinking in its collective head,
"Oh, well, just another nigga dead."

Cops copped a life of color!
A cat got capped by even cops of color who
Copped out and got co-opted into a corrupt conformity that
Consigns our kind to some crazy contumely,
Creating a contempt that ramps up
Amps to stamp out our community, and
Watts to swat our attempt to live humanly.

Yeah, I know that damn Goose made him kinda loose,
But that was no justification for an electronic noose!
They made it sound like he was in a threatening position
But that's another damn law enforcement fiction
'Cause eye witnesses made statements to the contrary.
But what I witness too often from the constabulary
Is a lack of emotional fitness to be carrying weaponry,
And a dangerous disposition to be the adversary.

And so, he was tasered.
You know—that "electronic control device" that's gotten
Out of control and is now the vice of choice for
Many an Out-of-control control freak.
That "non-lethal" weapon which
Seems to have been surprisingly lethal for the more than
300 people whose lives it's leaked!
I already had negative view about it;
I never thought this close to home the news would hit...

Checked my phone. Five times my sister had called?
Awwww, shit; something's wrong, yall!
Found out later. Too shocked to bawl,
Too stunned to cry. The guy who loved to run ball,
Whose smile was still so child-like on a man-child's body tall,
Was shocked and stunned to death,
Shrouded under hatred's pall.

The first baby boy of my sister.
How I wished I could be with her;
How more than ever I missed her.
I could only imagine her screams as her young mister
Which the Creator gifted her was ripped from her,
Creating a rift in her!
God, please uplift in her the strength to go on!

Took him to a game once.
Thank God for that one time—
Which he enjoyed and appreciated.
Let me know I wasn't hated
Even though my calls and cards were belated.
And though I rarely was around, he never berated.

Now, this is no excuse for it; it's nothing that makes it right.
But, admittedly, for a time his mother and
I weren't runnin' tight.
No, no, it's not like there was a fight, nothing deranged.
Just a brother and sister estranged—
Though that was beginning to change.

But, for many years, it was for no other reason than that
We hadn't sat down to talk.
Now we were in a season of tragedy that
Brought us into a closer walk.

Respect to my sis 'cause she always invited,
Always pleaded with me
To come get him and be that uncle I was supposed to be:
Spend time with him,
Be a man with him,
Encourage and, if need be, reprimand him.
Help him focus, teach him,
Give him some locus where he could reach in
And center himself, and execute his plans.
Now he's been executed by trigger-happy hands!

Weird, isn't it? Spend a career working with
Other people's kids
While your relationship with some of your own hits the skids,
Made slippery with good intentions.
So with all that having been mentioned,
Can't make the same mistake of absence with the next two;
Gotta honor Rel's memory, and to them be true.

Oh, internal investigations, of course, found no wrong doing
And, thus, no punitive action was ensuing.
Obviously they weren't really looking.
Too much a part of the system to make the correct booking.
The not-so-grand jury made no convictions.
The oppressors hope we lack conviction
And will wither in this war of attrition.
They act as if we owe them contrition!

But no, there will be no acquiescence to
The slavers' electronic whip!
No letting the memory of Jarrel and others slip!
No voltage that will leave our minds so dazed,
Our souls so tased,
That we accept this shit as just an unfortunate phase

And do nothing but merely turn the page
Or turn aside from our justified rage!
No, we won't let ourselves be consumed by hate,
But we don't appreciate the continued rate
At which our killers get to skate!
Too many folk have been charged and
Their murderers not charged!
Too many have been charged
While in the "authorities'" charge
And left twisted in some dying position
While those in charge get to hide
Behind their badges and positions.
So I charge us with the mission of unplugging the injustice
That kills our brothers and sisters,
That kills our children!

Shocking, but true.

So let's do what we gotta do:
Speak love to our children while we have the opportunity.
Speak truth to power to end police impunity.
We cannot and will not accept
This current recurrence of hate!
The survival of our families is at issue—
Indeed, the survival of our community.

And yo, 'Rel: I miss you.

Were you there when they crucified my Lord?
Were you there when they crucified my Lord?
Oh...
Sometimes it causes me to tremble, tremble, tremble.
Were you there when they crucified my Lord? [6]

Were you there? Did you see that shit?

People came from all around, like
Actors in some morbid tragedy
Taking their place at the place of the skull.
It was a hellified scene as the crowd swelled,
Hurling lynch-mob epithets and taking bets
As this radical organizer who posed a threat was
Hung up to dry.
A working-class brother getting' worked over.
And in the midst of the laughs and jeers, the cries and tears,
There was no rescue.
No cavalry at Calvary; naw, he was history.
He must have had Albert Sabo as a judge, and maybe
It was Pontius who piloted Mumia onto Death Row.

They had to take him out.
He should'a known they wouldn't go for no uppity nigger,
But I guess figured he was big and bad.
Maybe he spent too much time as a kid
With his cousins down south,
That Maat makin' him wanna change the world.
Mouthin' off to respectable folk.
Whippin' that behind in the temple!
Aw, hell naw—he done gone too far now!
Disrupting the cash flow. Impeding the avarice.
Should've stayed seen and not heard;
Now they strung him up for all to see—
Strange fruit hanging from Palestinian trees.

Did you see the nails?
No, not the four-inch kind you can get
100 to a box down at the hardware.
I'm talkin' about the ones the length of railroad spikes—
Almost as long as our excuses of
Why we can't be true disciples.
Each slam of the mallet was a ballot against
The self-determination of a people's soul.
They didn't want any *kujichagulia*.
They said "He' a damn troublemaker, and we'll
Free a thug off the street before we let him off the hook.
Let's nail this bastard!"

And so they did,
Stakes smashing through him,
his screams mixing with Mary's.
Like Richard and them sang:
"Can't you hear
The
Hammer ringing?!" [7]
I hear it ringing in my ears;
Can't get that sound out of my head!
I hear it every time some tortured one's found dead,
Our deadened souls having found no
Urgency in their distress calls. We call it distressing
That they should interrupt our church comfort
That we might comfort the afflicted and do justice that
Would have lifted them from under the oppressors' sword.
How untoward their effrontery. But now it's in front of me—
Millions of executions of God's children.
Our inaction says it loud and clear:
"Crucify them!"

And so they do,
With more than just a perfunctory piercing of the side.
Oh, there are electroshocks and beatings,
Decapitations with heads then used as soccer balls,
Waterboardings and castrations and burnings,
And all manner of things! Whatever sordid imaginations—

Or the US training manual—can come up with.
There are even slow deaths caused by heavy metals
Placed in communities of children of color,
Or crop prices corrupted by NAFTA
Making families have to starve at home,
Burn in the desert or get exploited up here.

The tormentors know exactly what the hell they're doing,
Feigning innocence while veiling their insolence and
Deigning it proper for folk to offer them forgiveness
For giving them this Gehenna when they themselves have
No plans to cease or desist.
Some wallow in some comfortable ignorance,
So much of the significance of the cross having been
Lost in their own self-serving salvation schemes
Sans any sense of the Struggle.
They snuggle in snide security while
The least of these are subjected to sorrow,
Stuck in surreal scenes so stripped of
Any semblance of the sacred
That they find themselves asking,
"My God, my God,
Why'd you leave us hangin'?"

Actually, we're the ones who are missing—
But how can the God in me greet the God in you
If I've no sense of the communal God in we?
Good God, it's true:
We're losing that understanding of the village,
Tolerating the pillage of others.
"Aww—isn't it a shame what's happening to them.
Oh well; I'm good!"
The cock has long since crowed thrice
On our vice of complacency.
Too often we shun our collective agency. Damn, that's scary,
Like storm skies draping over us while
The curtain of self-righteousness
That covered us is rent in two.
Too much poison in religion has left me suffocating under
30

The weight of conservative bullshit so
My soul strains to lift up long enough for a gasp of air.
My desiccation is caused by
A lack of dedication to real progression and thus
My faith finds itself parched. I'm drying up,
I'm drying out, I...

...Thirst.
For the inner peace which a deceitful institution has
Stolen from so many, even my ministerial self.
For a conscious Church that doesn't content itself with charity
But craves justice and isn't craven about working toward it.

But at least I'm better off than those who thirst.
Yeah, dying due to the deprivation of H_2O,
More than just their souls being dehydrated.
The dearth of potable causing notable misery.
It should be no mystery that privatized greed
And multinational devilry add to ailments like
Dysentery, diarrhea and dengue causing the demise of
24 thousand toddlers a day! We preach living water;
Maybe we should advocate for some, too.

"Wonder working power in the blood."
I wonder how much more blood must be spilled before
We exercise the power the Creator's endowed us with to
Make this on earth as it is in heaven.
People ain't really prayin' that prayer with their lives.
"Oh, think twice: it's just another day
For you and me in paradise." [8]
And thus their paradigm has become
So individualistic that they
Forget those to their side when they come into their kingdom.
Good religious folk saying "Fuck you; save yourself!"
Rulers making others carry their cross—
Heavy, like the interest imposed on impoverished nations
As vulture capitalists gamble for
The clothes off people's backs.

"But it's OK," they tell us. "Just get saved!"
I wish somebody had saved us from those slave ships named
"Jesus" and "Hope"
That saved us for the highest bidder while we were
Made to lie in bitter conditions.
No one saved us from the sword about to sever our hands
If we didn't show them where the gold and silver were.
Don't step to me about how he's your savior while you
Save your privilege and savor schemes that
Sustain the systematic suffering of God's beloved.
Save it! Spare me your sanctimonious condescension!
Your backstabbing smirks are sickening in their simpering.
You want to show me
Your spiritual connection with the Nazarene?
Get serious about changing the conditions that cause the
Cruel situations from which people really need to be saved!
Those who twist the teaching teach us not to question why,
Saying, "Don't worry—it's for your sins Jesus died,
So just keep your head in the sky
And wait to understand it better by and by,"
Instead of exposing right now the intimidators' lies.

But look:
There's your son being sacrificed on the altar of imperialism!
Our "leaders" reap profits; you get the flag off the coffin.
Check it: that's your mother being
Raped by corporate carnivores confining her to
Some horrific maquiladora nightmare!
Each night she fears what the next day will bring,
Wondering if she'll ever be able to say,
"It is finished."

Mother, by your hands may we
Commit our spirits to each other!

Let's roll away the stoned-out mindset that
Drugs us into docility.
Let's resurrect our community!
A couple thousand years later and

We still haven't created the New Jerusalem?
No wonder people look at church folk and say,
"What's the use of 'em?" Too often we fail in action, and
Don't back up the words or the principle.
And like the young brother in that movie,
I can imagine Jesus asking:
"You mean I got my ass whipped for nothing?"
In the name of the one who died that day,
Let's make it a better Friday.

Oh...
Sometimes it causes me
To tremble, tremble, tremble.
Were you there...? [6]

1. King Jr., Martin L. Why We Can't Wait (Signet Classics Edition). New York: Signet, 2000.

2. Traditional. "Blow Your Trumpet, Gabriel".

3. Miller, Steve. "Fly Like an Eagle." Fly Like an Eagle. Capitol, 1976.

4. Green Acres (television show), Hee Haw (television show), CBS. Little House on the Prarie (television show), NBC. Smallville (television show), The WB/The CW.

5. Gershwin, Ira. "Let's Call the Whole Thing Off". Shall We Dance (film), 1937.

6. Traditional. "Were You There".

7. Smallwood, Richard. "Calvary". Persuaded. Verity, 2001.

8. Collins, Phil. "Another Day in Paradise". But Seriously. Atlantic, 1989.

About the Author

A veteran of various forms of public speaking, Analysis is a spoken word poet, a rad bookseller and minister, an educator and consultant, a self-diagnosed soccer addict and a lover of justice and human rights! He's featured and spotlighted at venues across New England and the Mid-Atlantic. A background in civil rights and economic justice, anti-apartheid and anti-racist organizing, secondary education, justice theory and ministry, and international travel manifests itself in his poetry—as does a love of radical history, family, and people in general. There's also a naughty side that comes out now and then! A native of Baltimore, Maryland, he studied Public Communication at the American University and holds a Master of Divinity degree from Howard University, from which he graduated with highest honors. Analysis is the host of Red Emma's Mother Earth Poetry Vibe, and a member of Simply Poetic Entertainment. His chap book of poetry, Somewhere Through the Haze, is a short collection of pieces on a variety of justice & human rights topics. Let him engage your audiences and groups through performances, addresses, workshops and consultancies that will encourage them, in dynamic ways, to raise their levels of critical analysis!

Email: analysisthepoet@gmail.com
https://www.facebook.com/analysisthepoet
Twitter @analysisthepoet
Instagram: @analysisthepoet